Judo
Nage-no-Kata

Ute Pfeiffer/Guenther Bauer

Judo
Nage-no-Kata

Throwing Techniques

Meyer & Meyer Sport

Original title: Judo Nage-no-Kata
© Aachen: Meyer & Meyer, 2008

Judo – Nage-no-Kata
British Library Cataloguing in Publication Data
A catalogue record for this book is available from the British Library

Judo – Nage-no-Kata
Ute Pfeiffer / Guenther Bauer
Maidenhead: Meyer & Meyer Sport (UK) Ltd., 2010
ISBN: 978-1-84126-280-2

© 2010 by Meyer & Meyer Sport (UK) Ltd.
Aachen, Adelaide, Auckland, Budapest, Cape Town, Graz, Indianapolis,
Maidenhead, Olten (CH), Singapore, Toronto
Member of the World
Sport Publishers' Association (WSPA)
www.w-s-p-a.org
Printed by: B.O.S.S Druck und Medien GmbH
ISBN: 978-1-84126-280-2
E-Mail: info@m-m-sports.com
www.m-m-sports.com

Introduction

Description of the Throws – Nage-no-Kata

Appendices

President of the German Judo Association – Peter Frese

For every Dan grading test, the Kata are an important element. The Kata are often considered to be the 'grammar' of the sport of Judo.

The Nage-no-Kata are the Kata that every Judoka must perform for the 1st Dan grading test.

Ute Pfeiffer and Guenther Bauer have been successful in making the Nage-no-Kata easy to understand with clear descriptions. *Nage-no-Kata* is a splendid addition to the lessons given by an experienced Kata instructor. The book also makes it possible for the student to train without an instructor because the many important details are described with an exact method and a lot of good photos.

I am sure that this book will be of invaluable help to many a student on his way through the grading test for the 1st Dan in Judo. I would like to thank Ute Pfeiffer and Guenther Bauer for the production of this wonderful training manual.

Peter Frese
President of the German Judo Association

Introduction

The grading test for the 1ˢᵗ Dan is a great challenge for most Judokas. This fact clearly has its roots in the learning and practicing of something quite new in the Judokas' training program.

Techniques that have been learned now have to be performed and demonstrated in an exact laid down sequence of movements. The posture of the body, the grips, the layout of the mat and many other elements of the techniques are all now laid out in a particular order.

In 1981, we both were there as candidates for the Dan belt learning the Nage-no-Kata for the first time. We therefore know from our own experience how strenuous it can be to work up a Kata independently. In order to be able to demonstrate a Kata in a masterly fashion, one has to devote a lot of time and additional training sessions to achieve it. However, getting to terms with a Kata as well as studying its laid down form must be an outstanding achievement for every Judoka and this will help him to understand the theory and basics of Judo.

In this book we are going to lay out the up-to-date lessons for newcomers to the Kata as well as Kata club instructors. We have kept the text as short as possible in favor of providing a large number of photos. The sequence of the movements is pictured in the photos and texts supplement them. A number of detailed shots also highlight the important points.

Despite the required basic form of a Kata, each Kata is an expression of one's own personality. Therefore, with this in mind, you will find that our Kata descriptions also carry our own signature that has been passed down to us by the experienced Judo instructors and experts who have advised us over the years.

We hope that this book will make the route to achieving the Kyu and Dan grading tests easier for many Judokas.

"A Kata should demonstrate both victory and defeat, where attack and defense are agreed in detail beforehand."

Kyozu Mifune (10th Dan Kodokan)

What does Kata mean?

Kata generally means 'the basic form'. In Judo and in the other martial arts, Kata means 'practicing the basics' or 'practicing that which is traditional.' While, on the one hand, in Randori (free fighting training) and in Shiai (competition) it is about carrying out and executing techniques in adverse situations, in Kata it is about carrying them out and executing them in ideal situations. Over the years, Judo techniques have been influenced and further developed by the competition scenario. The basis behind Kata is therefore to maintain the traditional and original form of the technique. Each Kata has its own theme. These can be throwing techniques, groundwork techniques, counter-throws or also self-defense techniques. Uke (the one being thrown) and Tori (the thrower) demonstrate the techniques flawlessly in a flowing, dynamic sequence of movements. Body posture, starting positions, sequence of steps, attack and defense are all as important as a good use of the area and the symmetry of movement. The Kata is greatly characterized by the calm and harmony exuding from its execution.

Overview of the Kata most used in today's sport of Judo

▌ Nage-no Kata (Form of throwing)

▌ Katame-no-Kata (Form of groundwork and holding techniques)

▌ Gonosen-no-Kata (Form of counterattack throws)

▌ Kime-no-Kata (Form of decision)

▌ Goshin-Jutsu-no-Kata (Form of self-defense)

▌ Juno-Kata (Form of 'softness' and suppleness)

▌ Itsutsu-no-Kata (Form of the five 'principles' or forces of nature)

▌ Koshiki-no-Kata (Form of the old techniques)

The technical and mental principles of Judo are embraced in the Kata. Jigoro Kano (1860-1938) – the founder of today's Judo – formulated two principles. All Judo techniques stem from these guiding principles.

1.　**"Sei-Ryoku-Zen-Yo" – the technical principle**
This calls for the "best possible use of the body and mental spirit" – often interpreted as "winning by giving in." This means not only using physical strength but also by using a spiritual and mental outlook.

2.　**"Ji-Ta-Kyo-Ei" – the moral principle**
This principle can be interpreted as "mutual support for mutual advance and mutual well-being". Here, the approach to life and coexistence is highlighted by the mutual support and understanding provided by people cooperating with each other. Judo contributes greatly to the development of the Judoka's personality.

The perfect execution of a Kata should reflect the Judo principles formulated by Jigoro Kano.

The Nage-no-Kata

The Nage-no-Kata – the forms of throwing – covers the throwing techniques in Judo. They are divided into five groups each consisting of three throwing techniques. The 15 throwing techniques are done on both sides of the body. Generally, the right-sided technique is done first followed immediately afterwards by executing the left-sided version (with the exception of Uki-goshi). Between the individual groups it is required that a short pause be taken, during which Tori and Uke adjust their Judogi and prepare themselves mentally for the next group.

In the Nage-no-Kata, Tori and Uke should have the same technical abilities. Uke changes his attack method each time and forces Tori always to react in a different way. Tori breaks off his attack at first, but then moves immediately into the attack movements, following on with them or moving into a different direction. Uke always attacks in earnest, and Tori acts decisively and forcefully. Unnecessary movement should be avoided.
The throws should be executed perfectly and dynamically and the overall picture must exude calmness and harmony.

The Nage-no-Kata are, generally speaking, the first Kata that the Judoka has to learn. By learning them, in addition to the technical principles of the specific throws, he also learns the general rules such as the greeting, body posture, how to walk and move etc., that are also relevant for the other Kata.

Fifteen throwing techniques in five groups have to be demonstrated:

1st Group: Te-waza (Hand Techniques)
Uki-otoshi, Seoi-nage, Kata-guruma

2nd Group: Koshi-waza (Hip Throws)
Uki-goshi, Harai-goshi, Tsuri-komi-goshi

3rd Group: Ashi-waza (Leg and Foot Techniques)
Okuri-ashi-barai, Sasae-tsuri-komi-ashi, Uchi-mata

4th Group: Ma-sutemi-waza ('Sacrificial Throws on the Back' Techniques)
Tomoe-nage, Ura-nage, Sumi-gaeshi

5th Group: Yoko-sutemi-waza ('Sacrificial Throws on the Side' Techniques)
Yoko-gake, Yoko-guruma, Uki-waza

The Layout of the Mat

It is important before you start performing Kata that you familiarize yourself with the layout of the mat. Good use of the area and the symmetry of a performance are important criteria and play an important role in the judging of the impression made by a Kata performance.

In the following description, as in later detailed presentations of the throws, we use an 8 x 8 m large mat. This size permits ideal conditions for the Kata and should be the one used by the candidate for a Dan grading test.

With an 8 x 8m mat, the internal green area measures 6 x 6 m. This is surrounded by a border in red, bringing the total size up to 8 x 8 m. Serving as a safety zone, there must be at least one row of green mats.

The throw on Uke must always occur inside the red zone. For this reason, the starting position will vary for the various throwing techniques. In Kata championships, a foot on the red area of the mat during the execution of a throw is penalized by the deduction of a point. Regarding this aspect, the graders in a Dan test often overlook the deduction and do not always penalize this foul. Nevertheless, the candidate should always try to keep within this ruling. However, Uke may not be thrown so that he lands outside the red extremities of the mat, neither in the grading test nor in a competition.

If the mat is only 6 x 6 m, the red border can be used so that preparation and the appropriate throw can be made. In this case, Tori and Uke stand outside the red border to make their greetings.

On the other hand, when you have a 10 x 10 m mat and you are both the normal size, you may have problems with your orientation. In this case the greetings should take place inside the red border so that the same conditions are achieved as actions used with an 8 x 8 m mat.

Overview of the Layout of the Mat

▌ Mat – size 8 x 8 m

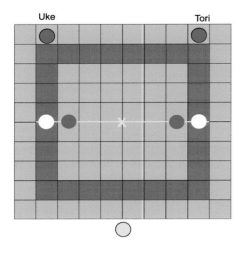

⬤ Waiting position prior to the start of a Kata performance

◯ Greeting

⬤ Position for adjustment of clothing

✕ Center of the mat

▬ The Kata axis

◯ Joseki

▌ Mat – size 10 x 10 m

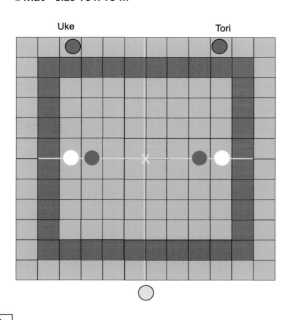

▌ Mat – size 6 x 6 m

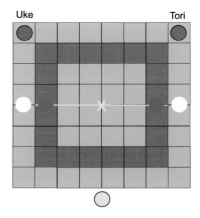

Joseki

The performance of the Kata takes place on the Joseki side of the mat – the side of honor. In a Dan grading test the judges sit on this side. In a Kata championship the referees also sit on this side. If the Kata is being demonstrated to a particularly interested audience then they should be sat down also on this side. In order to establish the starting positions for Tori and Uke, the first thing is to decide on which side of the mat the Joseki is.

In carrying out the initial and final greeting, Tori stands on the right-hand side and Uke stands on the left-hand side when looking from the Joseki position. In the pauses between the individual groups of throws, both Tori and Uke have the opportunity to adjust their Judogi. Seen from the Joseki side, these positions are for Tori on the right-hand side and for Uke on the left-hand side.

If Tori and Uke have to move to get to the next starting position after having executed a throw, they are both required to turn so that they do not show their backs to the Joseki side. Where, however, it is unavoidable because of the requirements of the Judo movements then there can be short exceptional instances when they will have their backs to the Joseki side.

The starting position for a left-sided throw, as seen from the Joseki side, is always a mirror image of the right-sided throw and is on the opposite side of the mat. In order to move to the new starting position, Tori and Uke should use as few steps as possible and whenever possible move at the same time.

Prior to the start of a Kata performance, Tori and Uke stand behind the red border area on the opposite side of the mat to the Joseki side – Tori to the right and Uke to the left. They wait here until the referee or the judge gives a sign that they may begin their demonstration. They both lead off with their left foot and move towards the Joseki side, parallel to each other until they reach the Kata axis. With a mat size of 8 x 8 m, Tori and Uke move down the red-bordered area.

The Kata Axis

The Kata axis is a straight line parallel to the Joseki side and dissects the center of the mat. Preparatory steps for a throw are mainly taken along this axis. The actual throw takes place mainly at the center of the mat.

An exception to this is the Okuri-ashi-barai. This throw is the only throw that takes place on an axis at right angles to the normal Kata axis. This line also goes through the center of the mat. For a right-sided throw Tori and Uke move away from the Joseki side, while for a left-sided throw they move towards the Joseki side.

The positions for the start and final greeting as well as the position for adjusting the Judogi are also on the Kata axis.

Tori and Uke

In Kata, Tori and Uke are equal partners. Both are responsible for the successful execution of the Kata demonstration.

Tori is the partner who carries out the technique – he does the throw. On the other hand, Uke attacks but gives way. This means that the technique is being carried out on him. Wherever possible, Uke should be a little taller than Tori.

In the course of the Kata, Uke should always give Tori new challenges by changing the direction of his attacks and/or changing his body posture. This way, Tori is forced to adapt to ever-changing situations and to react accordingly.

For Uke, it is important that he has learned how to fall well. He should show perfect body posture and control during a throw and when falling. When falling down, Uke must make sure that his feet are correctly placed. Using the hand to ward off the fall and lift the body forwards take place at the same time. In some throws, Uke comes out forwards from the Judo roll immediately into a stable, shoulder-width standing position.

Uke's attacks are done in earnest and are not feigned. Tori has to react straight away to Uke's attacks. To start with he gives way and then takes up and continues the attack movement. Tori uses Uke's impetus for his own defense i.e., throw. Uke allows this to happen, laying trust on Tori's throwing capabilities. Uke should not jump up to help the throw. Tori must be forceful, dynamic and nevertheless controlled without losing his balance. In the final position, following a throw, Tori should be standing stable on both feet and with his knees slightly bent. During the throw, Tori takes hold of Uke's arm in order to soften the fall.

Immediately from the start of the Kata and throughout, i.e. from the starting greeting and right up to the end of the technique and the final greeting, Tori and Uke should remain attentive and concentrated but not stiff.

Uke 受   Tori 取

Body Posture

When standing or walking, Tori and Uke keep their body posture upright. They look straight forward and pull their shoulders slightly back. The arms hang loosely down by their sides. The fingers are closed and almost point directly downwards. Thumbs are alongside the fingers and also are pointing downwards.

In the waiting posture when doing the starting and final greeting, Tori and Uke keep their feet close together with their feet spread out at a 60° angle. The heels are almost touching.

After the greeting, Tori and Uke take a deliberate step forward towards each other starting with the left foot and following on with the right foot. They now change the position of their feet to adopt the shoulder-width position. They remain with their feet like this throughout the whole demonstration of the throw.

Only at the conclusion of the performance do they then turn to face each other, adjust their clothing and now, in reverse order, place their right foot to the rear and then the left foot, leaving the shoulder-width foot position to come back into the closed foot position. This is then followed by the final greeting.

General Points

Moving – Walking

There is a difference made between moving/walking with-
out a partner and moving/
walking with a partner. The
following rule is made for
both types of movement. The
feet must keep touching the
floor, i.e. they do not quite
leave the mat surface. When
walking, only the heels are
raised up a little from the mat
while the toes and the sole of
the foot slides over the surface
of the mat.

Moving/Walking Without a Partner

When walking without a partner, one always leads with the left foot. The legs slide past each other
closely so that the feet pass by each other. Tori and Uke walk at a natural, easy pace without rushing.
The arms are hanging loosely down by the sides of the body and only swing a little or not at all.

Moving/Walking With a Partner

When walking with a partner, various steps are used depending on the different attacks being
used. These preparatory steps prior to throwing are described in detail in the instruction for the
throwing technique. In some of the Nage-no-Kata throws, Uke attacks using a sliding shuffle step
(feet sliding forwards). This type of movement is known also as 'Tsugi-ashi'. For this the feet do not
pass each other as they are slid forward. The movement is one where you don't necessarily have to
watch your balance, but one where your partner can push you over quite easily. The posture of the
body remains upright.

The sliding shuffle step form looks like this; Tori and Uke stand opposite each other with their feet
shoulder-width apart. The distance between them is about an arm's length. At the same time as he
applies a right-handed grip, Uke moves, leading with his right foot, towards Tori. Tori also attacks
and dodges back with his left foot. Uke follows this move by bringing his left foot up about level
with his right heel or center of the foot. Important: Uke's left foot must not go past his right. Tori,
who has dodged back with his left foot, pulls his right foot until it is level with the middle of his left
foot. As with Uke, the same applies to Tori who must not let his right foot pass his left foot that he
placed to the rear earlier. The second sliding shuffle step takes place now but is done a
little faster.

When Uke has taken a third sliding shuffle step, Tori should have got him clearly off-balance so that Tori can use his third step to start the throw.

Because the sliding shuffle step footwork for a throw will be executed quicker, there is an acceleration of the movements until the high point is reached resulting in a dynamically executed throw.

When walking, care must be taken to keep the shoulders always at about the same height and to keep them from waving up and down. The steps should be done in a flowing movement and not jerked.

After completion of a right-sided throw, Tori and Uke stay in the final position for a moment or two. They then loosen their grip and return to the starting position again in order to execute the left-sided throw, using as few steps as possible.

Tori and Uke must take care that they do not turn their backs to the Joseki side, while the movements they make must be as uncomplicated and as natural as possible. The sliding shuffle step footwork for the left-sided throw is a mirror image of the right-sided throw. The words 'right' and 'left' just have to be changed over.

Tsugi-ashi Footwork

The Defensive Posture (Jigotai)

For the **Sumi-gaeshi** and the **Uki-waza**, Tori and Uke adopt a right sided or left-sided defensive posture (Migi-jigotai/Hidari-jigotai). The body posture and grip positions are the same for both. Tori and Uke stand opposite each other about 1m apart. Leading with the right foot, both move towards each other for the right-sided throw and attack at the same time. Feet are well apart and the center of balance is kept low. The knees are bent and point outwards. The right hand is pushed through underneath the partner's armpit and is placed on his shoulder blade. The left hand grabs hold of the upper arm just above the elbow (not the Judogi).

A rounded position of the arm is achieved by lifting the elbow up to shoulder height. The upper bodies are upright but with the center of balance a little towards the rear. A firm grip is required in order to maintain the pressure. The next step taken is done in a circular motion. Tori pulls Uke forcibly forwards with his right hand and at the same time brings his right foot back in a circular motion. So that he doesn't lose his balance, Uke has to move towards Tori in a circular motion with his left foot. Tori and Uke are now standing in the defensive posture facing each other. The next step has specifically to do with the throw and will be described later when we go through the throwing techniques.

Defensive Posture

The Grip/Attack

Tori and Uke take up the starting positions for the next throw and pause for a while in this position. For each throw Uke always takes the attacking initiative. By changing the direction of thrusts or by varying his body posture, he uses different attack forms. He learns from his mistakes and the Kata slowly develop from this. Tori is confronted every time with new actions and has to react accordingly. In the following description of a throw, Uke's attacks and Tori's reactions to them are gone into in detail.

Other than a few exceptions, Tori and Uke attack each other using the normal arm and collar grip. For the right-sided throw, both grab hold of the other's left lapel at the height of the collarbone, while the left hand grabs hold of the sleeve of the jacket just above the right elbow. For a left-handed throw, the holds are changed over.

At the same time as the grips are applied, Uke moves towards Tori for most of the throws by using the **Tsugi-ashi** footwork steps. Because he is forced to move backwards, Tori also uses this form to dodge rearwards away from Uke's attack.

In the **Tsuri-komi-goshi**, Tori changes the form of his grip right from the beginning and with his right hand he grabs hold of the shoulder of Uke's jacket, and not the lapel. This form of grip allows him to push his partner upwards. In an upright body position, this movement will pull Uke forward clearly off balance.

The **Sumi-gaeshi** and **Uki-waza** throws are done from the defensive posture. For this Tori and Uke both change their holding grips. Both push their right hand through underneath the left armpit of the other partner. The open hand is then laid on the other's shoulder blade area.

The left hand grabs hold of the partner's upper arm (not the Judogi) just above the elbow. By angling the arms and lifting the elbow up to shoulder height, Tori and Uke achieve a rounded-arm position.

Both attempt to push the other off balance by deliberately pushing forwards without losing their own balance. In order to hold the pressure of the grip, Tori and Uke must apply a very firm grip.

The Punching Attack

For the techniques of the **Seoi-nage, Uki-goshi** and **Yoko-guruma**, Uke attacks using a punch downwards on Tori's head. This is done with Tori and Uke about 2 m apart opposite each other.

When doing the right-handed version, first of all Uke takes a step forward with the left foot towards Tori and swings his closed right fist back for the punch. His left hand is also closed and formed into a fist held as a defense in front of his body.

Uke's next step is to move forward with his right foot and at the same time target his punch at Tori's head. In order to understand the method of this punching attack, think of the arm and body position required when trying to throw a ball a long way.

The punch must be done forcefully but under control so that Tori can use the attack and exploit it. For the four punching attacks, Uke should vary his body posture so that he can hinder being thrown by the same throw each time.

So that Tori can remain standing stable and upright after a throw, Uke should only hold onto Tori's jacket for as long as it is particularly necessary. In order to assist Uke as he falls, Tori grabs hold of the arm of Uke's jacket with both hands during the throw and holds on until the end position is reached.

Arranging the Clothing

Tori's and Uke's Judogi should naturally be clean and they should be wearing the correct size. Clothing that is too close a fit is not suitable. The arms of the jacket should reach down to the wrists and the legs of the pants down to the ankles. Both partners tie their belt really tight and firmly.

By doing this they make sure that as far as possible, when doing the throwing techniques, their clothing does not get too out of shape and disarranged.

In accordance with tradition, for Kata championships and Dan grading tests, both partners have to wear white Judogi. However, in this book, so that the difference is quite clear, we have put Tori in white and Uke in blue Judo gear.

Between the individual throwing groups, Tori and Uke have the opportunity to rearrange their Judogi. After every third left-sided throw of each group, they go to the position for adjusting their clothing.

By this we mean the position where they were after they took up the starting positions after the greeting.

They stand for a short while, feet shoulder-width apart looking outwards. When both are in place, they begin to adjust their clothing. The jacket can be easily straightened by taking hold of the bottom corners – the right hand holds the left-hand bottom end and the left hand holds the right-hand bottom end and they are pulled sharply downwards. So that they then turn towards each other at the same moment, Tori and Uke should count together silently a figure agreed between 5-10 seconds, and then turn. To practice this at the beginning they may count out loud, but at later stages they should do it silently.

Using acoustic signs like snapping the belt or making similar sounds should be avoided in Kata performances. They are unnecessary and tend to disturb rather than help.

At the end of the short pause while they arrange their clothing, they turn towards each other again. So that they don't turn their backs to the Joseki side, Tori turns to the right and Uke to the left. They should do this synchronized and in unison. After a short moment in this position, they can start the execution of the next throwing group.

The Phases of the Throwing Technique

The Attack

Uke begins the attack by grabbing hold of Tori's Judogi and moving towards him at the same time – alternatively Uke might use a punching attack. Attacks are done forcefully. Uke learns from his mistakes and changes his direction of attack or his body posture each time.

The Reaction

Tori reacts to Uke's attack by giving way, picking up the impetus of the attack and exploiting it or by diverting the attack direction for his own good. For a throw, it is necessary for Tori to change his grip. This phase of the preparation for the throw must be visible to the testers or judges.

Loss of Balance (Kuzushi)

The moment when the balance is lost is a basic requirement for the success of a throw in Judo. In this phase, Tori must get Uke into such an off-balance situation by appropriately pulling, pushing or lifting him. Uke's loss of balance must be clearly visible but achieved without any time being lost.

Preparing to Throw (Tsukuri)

Having broken Uke's balance, Tori maneuvers himself into the correct position to execute the throw. The aim of the throw preparation is the throw itself. It must be executed with technical perfection and without Tori losing his own balance.

Execution (Kake)

The steps being taken by Tori and Uke should form a flowing movement at a good pace and with increasing dynamics. The execution of the throw is the highpoint of the sequence of movements.

Once executed, both pause for a while in the end position and then move calmly and deliberately to the next starting position. Tori and Uke have to ensure that the impression given is one of a harmonically executed sequence of movements.

Overview of the Throwing Groups

1st Group:	Te-waza (Hand Techniques)

Uki-otoshi	Seoi-nage	Kata-guruma

2nd Group:	Koshi-waza (Hip Throws)

Uki-goshi	Harai-goshi	Tsuri-komi-goshi

3rd Group:	Ashi-waza (Leg and Foot Techniques)

Okuri-ashi-barai	Sasae-tsuri-komi-ashi	Uchi-mata

4th Group:	Ma-sutemi-waza ('Sacrificial Throws on the Back' Techniques)

Tomoe-nage   Ura-nage   Sumi-gaeshi

5th Group:	Yoko-sutemi-waza ('Sacrificial Throws on the Side' Techniques)

Yoko-gake   Yoko-guruma   Uki-waza

Instructions for the Descriptions of the Throws

The Right-Sided Throw

The throws on the right side of the body (with the exception of Uki-goshi) are each depicted on two pages using seven photos and comprehensive texts.

Photo 1 shows the starting position for the throw. The applicable text for this photo is just to the right of it.

Photos 2-7 are in the center of the page and are slightly diagonally aligned. They show the sequence of movements from the attack through the preparation for the throw and the loss of balance phase up to the actual throw itself. The text below each photo describes the sequence.

Circular 'zoom' photos highlight the important points. These are described clearly in the boxes labeled 'Detail'.

Along the bottom border of the pages – once to the left-hand page and once to the right of the second (right-hand page) are small birds-eye diagrams of the Judo mat. The situation at the start is shown in the left hand one, and the end situation is shown in the right hand one.

Starting Position

Detail Zoom Photos

Sequence – Right-Sided Throw

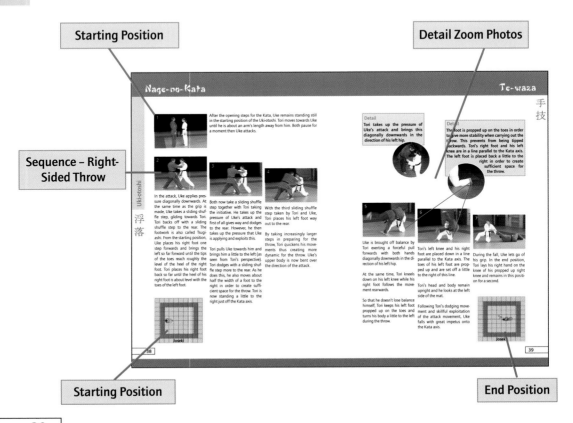

Starting Position

End Position

The Left-Sided Throw

On the next set of two pages, the first row of photos (Photos 1-6) show – left to right – the transition to the left-sided throw. The photos are described in the text immediately below them.

Both of the next rows of photos show the movements and they have to be followed from right to left. This representation may seem a little strange to start with, but it was important for us that we showed the sequence of movements as clearly as possible.

To aid reading we have numbered the photos and indicated the order to be read by inserting arrows.

The photos in the middle row (Photos 7-12) show the sequence of movements for the left-sided throw. It is a mirror image of the movements for the right-sided throw. Therefore we have done away with any description of the throw itself. The words 'right' and 'left' just have to be changed over in the mind for the left-sided throw.

The transition to the next throwing technique is depicted in Photos 13-18 together with descriptive text.

Starting with the greeting and ending with the final parting bow, the series of photos show an almost continuous depiction of the Nage-no-Kata.

Transition to the Left-Sided Throw

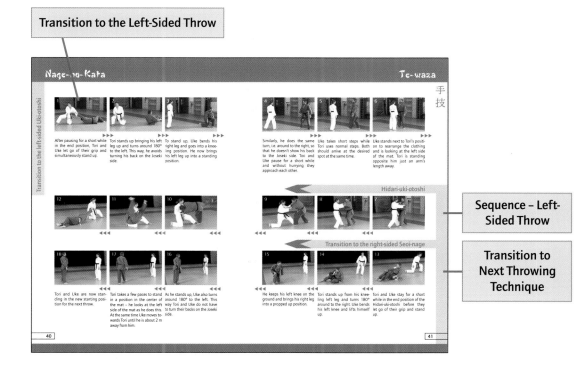

Sequence – Left-Sided Throw

Transition to Next Throwing Technique

Description of the Throws – Nage-no-Kata

The Greeting

Tori and Uke adopt an upright standing posture. They both look straight ahead. Their arms are hanging loosely by the sides of their bodies. The fingers are closed together and are almost stretched downwards. Tori's and Uke's feet are close together with the heels almost touching. The feet point outwards at an angle of 60°. Tori and Uke have to wait until the examiner or a judge gives a sign that they may start their demonstration. **(Photo 1)**

As soon as the sign has been given, leading with the left foot, both move at the same time to the Kata axis. Tori and Uke try to move synchronously. Once they reach the Kata axis, they pause for a second and bow towards the Joseki side. As they do this, their hands glide around from the side of the body and onto and down the thighs until the tips of the fingers reach the knees. The head follows the movement of the upper body and they look downwards at the mat for a short period. **(Photo 2)**

Tori and Uke stand upright again. The hands glide back from the thighs to the sides of the body. They look straight ahead and the closed feet position is maintained. **(Photo 3)**

►►►

Both now turn towards each other. Tori turns to his right and Uke to his left. Both are standing on the Kata axis. **(Photo 4)**

Tori and Uke now kneel down and bow towards each other. First of all, each places his left foot so far to the rear so that when the left knee is on the ground it is roughly level with the right foot on the mat. **(Photo 5)**

Immediately after, the right knee is placed parallel to the other. For a short period, both Tori and Uke are now kneeling. The feet remain propped up on the toes. **(Photo 6)**

They now stretch their toes back out while the feet stay together (i.e., not crossed over). They sit down on their heels/lower legs. The knees are about two widths of the hand apart. At the same time, Tori and Uke take hold of the ends of their belt and lay them outwards. The hands then glide back on to the thighs. The tip of each hand points together. Both hold their head and upper body upright and the shoulders are slightly pulled back. **(Photo 7)**

After a short pause both bow towards each other. As they do this, their hands glide down from the thighs until they are in front of the knees and form a triangle on the mat. The tips of the fingers of each hand do not touch each other but are about 10 cm apart. The upper body follows this movement. The bottom, however, must not leave the heels. Head and upper body form a line so that they are looking at their hands. **(Photo 8)**

After a short time both lift themselves back up. Their hands glide back on to their thighs. The sequence of movements to stand back up again is the opposite of that when they kneeled down. Tori and Uke kneel up on one knee and prop their toes back up again. The hands stay on their thighs. **(Photo 9)**

▶▶▶

To stand up, first they bring their right foot forward and then the left one. Tori and Uke are now standing upright opposite each other with their feet in the closed position. The arms are now hanging loosely by their sides again. **(Photo 10)**

The Kata now starts in earnest – the opening steps are taken. Tori and Uke approach each other with deliberate steps leading first with the left foot followed by the right foot. The footwork must appear deliberate, but not looking as if they were surmounting an obstacle. Tori and Uke now change over from a closed foot position – as with the greeting – into a shoulder-width position. **(Photo 11)**

The greeting is now over. Both stand about half a meter inside the red border of the mat. After each throwing group is completed, this position is where they carry out the arrangement of their clothing. **(Photo 12)**

1st Group:
Te-waza (Hand Techniques)

▌ Uki-otoshi
▌ Seoi-nage
▌ Kata-guruma

Uki-otoshi

Seoi-nage

Kata-guruma

浮
落

After the opening steps for the Kata, Uke remains standing still in the starting position of the Uki-otoshi. Tori moves towards Uke until he is about an arm's length away from him. Both pause for a moment then Uke attacks.

In the attack, Uke applies pressure diagonally downwards. At the same time as the grip is made, Uke takes a sliding shuffle step, gliding towards Tori. Tori backs off with a sliding shuffle step to the rear. The footwork is also called Tsugi-ashi. From the starting position, Uke places his right foot one step forwards and brings the left so far forward until the tips of the toes reach roughly the level of the heel of the right foot. Tori places his right foot back so far until the heel of his right foot is about level with the toes of the left foot.

Both now take a sliding shuffle step together with Tori taking the initiative. He takes up the pressure of Uke's attack and first of all gives way and dodges to the rear. However, he then takes up the pressure that Uke is applying and exploits this.

Tori pulls Uke towards him and brings him a little to the left (as seen from Tori's perspective). Tori dodges with a sliding shuffle step more to the rear. As he does this, he also moves about half the width of a foot to the right in order to create sufficient space for the throw. Tori is now standing a little to the right just off the Kata axis.

With the third sliding shuffle step taken by Tori and Uke, Tori places his left foot way out to the rear.

By taking increasingly larger steps in preparing for the throw, Tori quickens his movements thus creating more dynamic for the throw. Uke's upper body is now bent over in the direction of the attack.

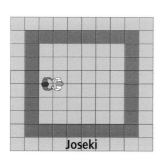

Joseki

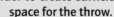

Detail

Tori takes up the pressure of Uke's attack and brings this diagonally downwards in the direction of his left hip.

Detail

The foot is propped up on the toes in order to give more stability when carrying out the throw. This prevents being tipped backwards. Tori's right foot and his left knee are in a line parallel to the Kata axis. The left foot is placed back a little to the right in order to create sufficient space for the throw.

5

6

7

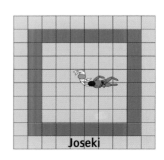

Uke is brought off balance by Tori exerting a forceful pull forwards with both hands diagonally downwards in the direction of his left hip.

At the same time, Tori kneels down on his left knee while his right foot follows the movement rearwards.

So that he doesn't lose balance himself, Tori keeps his left foot propped up on the toes and turns his body a little to the left during the throw.

Tori's left knee and his right foot are placed down in a line parallel to the Kata axis. The toes of his left foot are propped up and are set off a little to the right of this line.

Tori's head and body remain upright and he looks at the left side of the mat.

Following Tori's dodging movement and skillful exploitation of the attack movement, Uke falls with great impetus onto the Kata axis.

During the fall, Uke lets go of his grip. In the end position, Tori lays his right hand on the knee of his propped up right knee and remains in this position for a second.

Joseki

▶▶▶ ▶▶▶ ▶▶▶

After pausing for a short while in the end position, Tori and Uke let go of their grip and simultaneously stand up.

Tori stands up bringing his left leg up and turns around 180° to the left. This way, he avoids turning his back on the Joseki side.

To stand up, Uke bends his right leg and goes into a kneeling position. He now brings his left leg up into a standing position.

◀◀◀ ◀◀◀ ◀◀◀

◀◀◀ ◀◀◀ ◀◀◀

Tori and Uke are now standing in the new starting position for the next throw.

Tori takes a few paces to stand in a position in the center of the mat – he looks at the left side of the mat as he does this. At the same time Uke moves towards Tori until he is about 2 m away from him.

As he stands up, Uke also turns around 180° to the left. This way Tori and Uke do not have to turn their backs on the Joseki side.

▶▶▶   ▶▶▶   ▶▶▶

Similarly, he does the same turn, i.e. around to the right, so that he doesn't show his back to the Joseki side. Tori and Uke pause for a short while and without hurrying they approach each other.

Uke takes short steps while Tori uses normal steps. Both should arrive at the desired spot at the same time.

Uke stands next to Tori's position to rearrange the clothing and is looking at the left side of the mat. Tori is standing opposite him just an arm's length away.

Hidari-uki-otoshi

◀◀◀   ◀◀◀   ◀◀◀

Transition to the right-sided Seoi-nage

◀◀◀   ◀◀◀   ◀◀◀

He keeps his left knee on the ground and brings his right leg into a propped up position.

Tori stands up from his left leg and turns 180° around to the right. Uke bends his left knee and lifts himself up.

Tori and Uke stay for a short while in the end position of the Hidari-uki-otoshi before they let go of their grip and stand up.

Seoi-nage

背負投

For the starting position of the Seoi-nage, Tori and Uke stand 2 m apart from each other. Both are standing on the Kata axis, Tori in the center of the mat.

Uke takes a step forwards with his left foot and at the same time pulls his closed right fist back for the punch.

He holds his left hand clinched into a fist in front of his body as a defense. Uke's deliberate attack targets Tori's head.

> **Detail**
>
> Tori takes hold of Uke's attacking arm on the inside. The left hand grabs hold of Uke's upper arm just above the elbow (not the Judogi).

Uke now takes a second step. He moves towards Tori leading with his right foot and delivers a hammer punch down on Tori's head.

At the same time Tori places his right foot diagonally forwards. He lifts his left hand up as if to grab the punching arm coming down but without blocking it.

As Uke completes his punch, Tori grabs hold of Uke's upper arm on the inside, just above the elbow, and diverts the punch away a little towards the outside.

Tori ends the start phase of the throw by bringing his left foot backwards in order to be standing parallel in front of Uke. His knees are a little bent and his hips are underneath Uke's center of balance.

At the same time as the end of the start phase for the throw, Tori's right arm reaches through right underneath Uke's punching arm so that Tori's right shoulder is under Uke's right armpit. Tori's right hand is lying on Uke's shoulder.

The Judogi is not held on to during these actions.

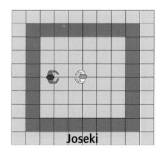

Joseki

Detail

Uke's punching arm is held just above the elbow (locked grip) and pulled forward. Tori's left hand is holding the upper arm and not the Judogi. Tori's right hand is pushed through underneath Uke's armpit and is laid on Uke's shoulder. Tori's right shoulder is tucked up tightly under Uke's armpit giving fully controlled contact with the shoulder.

Detail

Uke has moved up to Tori with his left foot and is now standing parallel behind Tori. He tries to defend himself against the throw by thrusting against Tori's back about the height of the belt.

5

Uke moves further with his left leg so that he is parallel behind Tori. He tries for the last time to prevent being thrown by thrusting his left hand at Tori's back at about the height of the belt.

However, Tori takes up the impetus of the punching action and brings his attack on further forwards. By doing so he brings Uke off balance.

6

By leaning his upper body forwards, turning slightly to the left and stretching his legs up, Tori throws his partner over his right shoulder.

7

Uke falls down along the Kata axis in front of Tori's feet. Tori grabs hold of the sleeve with his right hand and stands up.

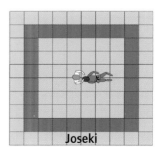

Joseki

43

Transition to the left-sided Seoi-nage

▶▶▶

▶▶▶

▶▶▶

After a short pause, Tori and Uke let go of their grip.

Uke now bends his left leg and brings his right foot up.

Uke brings his right leg up to stand up and moves along the Kata axis to the right side of the mat without pausing.

◀◀◀

◀◀◀

◀◀◀

◀◀◀

◀◀◀

◀◀◀

Tori and Uke stand opposite each other with legs shoulder-width apart. In an ideal situation, both arrive at the new starting position at the same time.

While this is happening, Tori reaches a position about an arm's length away from Uke.

Having reached the left side of the mat, roughly in the area where the rearrangement of clothing is carried out, Uke turns 180° around to the left.

▶▶▶   ▶▶▶   ▶▶▶

At the same time Tori adjusts his position. In most cases, two paces suffice in order to reach the center of the mat, thus coming into the starting position for the Hidari-seoi-nage.

At a distance of about 2 m from the center of the mat, Uke turns around to the right so that he doesn't turn his back on the Joseki side.

From a 'Joseki' perspective, Uke is standing on the right side of the mat looking at Tori.

Hidari-seoi-nage

◀◀◀   ◀◀◀   ◀◀◀

Transition to the right-sided Kata-guruma

◀◀◀   ◀◀◀   ◀◀◀

Ideally, Tori and Uke move synchronically with each other. Movements between the throws should be done harmoniously and deliberately. Unnecessary steps should be left out.

He stands up by bringing his right leg up and goes along the Kata axis to the left side of the mat. Tori waits until Uke has stood up and then follows him in step.

Tori and Uke pause for a second in the end position of the Hidari-seoi-nage before they let go of their grip. First of all, Uke stands up by bending his right knee and placing his left foot down.

45

Kata-guruma

肩車

For the starting position of the Kata-guruma, Uke is standing at the point where clothing is rearranged. Tori is opposite him and they are about an arm's length apart from each other. After a short pause Uke attacks.

Uke's attack comes from an upright position. Gripping normally, Uke pushes forwards and diagonally upwards.

At the same time as he is applying the grip, Uke takes a sliding shuffle step towards Tori leading with his right foot followed up by his left foot being pulled forward.

Tori grabs hold as well and yields backward with the corresponding step sequence.

With the second sliding shuffle step, Tori puts his left hand through inside and underneath Uke's arm and grabs hold of Uke's Judogi at about upper arm height.

He takes on the impetus of Uke's attack and pulls himself diagonally upwards in the direction of the pressure from Uke's attack. Tori has to maintain the pull he is exerting with his left hand until he executes the throw.

In Tori's third step, that is considerably larger than others, he turns his left foot to the left. The right foot follows the turning movement, but stays more or less on the spot. By pulling harder upwards and diagonally, Uke is brought off balance.

Uke is stretched right up and is standing merely on his right forefoot.

Standing up with his body slightly inclined to the right, Tori bends his knees in order to get underneath Uke's center of balance. Tori grasps forward through in between Uke's legs and holds him around the thighs. For this the hand is merely laid on the thigh and is not grasping the leg of the pants.

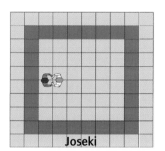

Joseki

Detail

Uke doesn't let his body hang over backwards, but supports himself by placing his left hand on Tori's back at about shoulder blade height. In this way he prevents himself from being thrown over backwards. Uke lies stretched out on Tori's shoulders. Uke keeps his body tensed and this aids Tori's lift and throw.

Detail

In order to fall easier and safer, Uke bends his right arm and grabs hold of Tori's left arm from below at about elbow height.

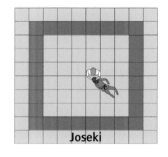

5

The left-handed pull is kept up constantly and makes for a flowing movement as Tori picks up Uke.

Tori places his right shoulder against Uke's right side between the belt and the groin. Tori lifts Uke up by lifting up his upper body that is inclined to the right and stretching up from the knees.

Uke supports himself with his left hand held on Tori's back and stretched out on Tori's shoulders. This way he can prevent being thrown backwards.

6

Without a pause, Uke is thrown in a rounded, flowing movement by continually pulling with the arm and with support from the right arm. As he does this, Tori keeps his right foot firmly on the ground and brings his left foot out until he is standing with feet shoulder-width apart.

The feet should not be too close together, otherwise Tori will not have such a stable stance.

Uke is thrown about 45° to the Kata axis. During the throw, Uke bends his right arm and grabs hold of Tori's left arm from underneath at elbow height. Uke falls down in a stretched out position.

7

During the throw, Tori grabs hold of the right sleeve of Uke's jacket with his right hand so that Uke lands safely on the left side of his body.

Joseki

▶▶▶   ▶▶▶   ▶▶▶

Tori and Uke stay for a short while in the end position before they let go of their grip.

Uke stands up again coming up from his left knee by pushing out his right foot and first of all bending his left leg.

As this is happening, Tori turns 90° to the left and now looks at the right side of the mat. Uke stands up bringing his left knee up.

◀◀◀   ◀◀◀   ◀◀◀

◀◀◀   ◀◀◀   ◀◀◀

Tori and Uke are now standing about 2 m apart.

When turning around Uke has already corrected his position and is standing about 1 m inside the red border of the mat. Tori moves to the center of the mat towards Uke leading with his left foot.

During this, they count to themselves the agreed number of seconds (5-10 seconds) and then turn around simultaneously towards each other. Tori turns to his right and Uke turns to his left. Looking at each other, both are now standing opposite each other.

▶▶▶   ▶▶▶   ▶▶▶

He now goes along the Kata axis to the right side of the mat. In step with Uke, Tori also moves to the right side.

At about the position for the adjustment of the clothing of Tori, Uke turns around 180° to the right and stands feet shoulder-width apart looking at Tori. At the same time Tori moves up towards Uke and stands a short arm's length away from him.

Tori and Uke have to coordinate their footwork so that both arrive at the new starting position at the same time.

Hidari-kata-guruma

◀◀◀   ◀◀◀   ◀◀◀

Transition to the left-sided Uki-goshi

◀◀◀   ◀◀◀   ◀◀◀

Looking outwards, Uke also stays on the spot where the clothing is adjusted. If their Judogi have become disarranged, both have an opportunity here to adjust it.

He stands up by bringing his left leg up and goes to the left side of the mat. At the same time Tori turns 90° to the left and goes to the right side of the mat and remains looking outwards.

After a short pause in the end position, Tori and Uke let go of their grip. Because the end of the first group of throws has now been reached, Tori and Uke move to the position where the clothing is adjusted. Uke bends his right leg, preparing to stand up.

49

2nd Group:
Koshi-waza (Hip Throws)

- Uki-goshi
- Harai-goshi
- Tsuri-komi-goshi

Uki-goshi

Harai-goshi

Tsuri-komi-goshi

浮
腰

Tori stands in the center of the mat for the Hidari-uki-goshi. Uke stands about 2m opposite him. This distance is necessary to allow for Uke's punching attack.

This can be varied according to body size.

> **Detail**
> **Tori grasps right around Uke's hips with his left arm.**

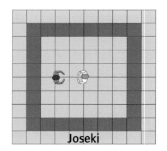

As an exception, the Uki-goshi is executed first of all with a left-sided throw. Accordingly, Uke attacks with a right-handed fist punch.

First of all, he takes a large step forward with his left foot. At the same time he pulls back his clenched right fist and holds his left hand – also clenched in a fist – as defense in front of his body.

As a second step, Uke moves his right leg forward. At the same time he brings his right arm high upwards in order to complete the punch on Tori's head.

Differently to the Seoi-nage, here Uke is attacking in an upright posture.

Simultaneously, Tori moves towards his partner by placing his left foot diagonally forwards.

He grasps right around Uke's hips with his left arm and pulls him towards his body. Using the left hip and the side of his body he blocks Uke at about belt height (contact with the side of the hip and stomach) and stops Uke's forward movement abruptly.

As he blocks, Tori is standing turned at an angle of about 90° in front of Uke. Keeping his body still upright, Uke places his left foot forwards.

Uke is now standing with feet parallel about shoulder-width apart.

Joseki

Detail

Uke's left upper arm is being gripped just above the elbow (not by the Judogi).

Detail

Position of the feet for the Uki-goshi left-sided throw.

Tori now moves fully into the throw by placing his right leg to the rear in a large semi-circular motion.

His left leg is between Uke's legs and his right leg is placed to the right on the outside of Uke's legs.

Tori's and Uke's feet are parallel to each other.

At the same time, Tori grips Uke's upper arm above the elbow with his right hand and pulls him to the right.

Uke is now off balance in this position.

Uke completes his punch, but it comes down past Tori's back.

Tori twists Uke over his hip by rotating Uke's body along the body axis. As he does this, Tori turns his head and upper body as far as possible to the right, in order to give the necessary impetus and space for the throw

If the body movement isn't carried out correctly, this usually leads to Uke landing to Tori's left and not on the Kata axis as is intended.

Uke lands ideally on the Kata axis.

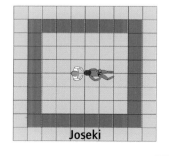

Joseki

Tori and Uke stay for a short pause before they let go of their grip.

Uke stands up again coming up from his right knee by bending it bringing his left leg up to a standing position.

The left leg is stretched out for this. While Uke is standing up Tori has already adjusted his position.

Tori and Uke ideally reach the starting position for the next throw at the same time.

About 1 m before he reaches the red border of the mat, Uke turns around to the left 180° and stands with his feet shoulder-width apart. As Uke turns, Tori takes a last step towards him and is now standing just about an arm's length from Uke.

Tori gets into step with Uke and follows him at a reasonable distance so that the sequence of movements appears harmonious.

▶▶▶   ▶▶▶   ▶▶▶

He now moves leading with the left foot straight ahead to the center of the mat. Meanwhile Uke moves along the Kata axis to the right side of the mat.

About 1 m before he reaches the red border of the mat, Uke turns around to the right 180°.

Tori and Uke are now standing, feet shoulder-width apart about 2 m away from each other.

Right Uki-goshi

◀◀◀   ◀◀◀   ◀◀◀

Transition to the right-sided Harai-goshi

◀◀◀   ◀◀◀   ◀◀◀

Uke is now standing up and moves along the Kata axis to the left side of the mat.

He stands up bringing his left knee up.

After a successful throw Tori and Uke remain for a short while in the end position before they let go of their grip. Uke stands up by bending his left knee and bringing his right leg up.

The starting position for the Harai-goshi is on the left side of the mat. Uke is standing on the spot where the rearrangement of clothing is carried out with Tori opposite him. The distance between Tori and Uke is just about an arm's length. Both pause for a second and then Uke attacks.

Detail

With his third step, Tori turns his left foot 180° around to the left and places it down in the direction of the throw.

Uke exerts pressure directly forwards. The attack is done with the body upright.

Tori dodges back from Uke's pressure and sliding shuffle step (Tsugi-ashi) also by doing a sliding shuffle step to the rear.

As they both do the second sliding shuffle step, Tori attacks with the right hand, pushing it through under Uke's left armpit and places his hand on Uke's shoulder blade.

Tori exploits the impetus of Uke's attack and increases the pull on Uke's right arm.

At the same time, Tori pulls Uke with his right hand towards his body and slightly upwards. Tori's right hand is not grasping the Judogi, but remains lying flat on the shoulder blade also during the throw.

Uke takes a further third sliding shuffle step towards Tori. At the same time, Tori takes his third step.

As he moves into the rearwards movement, he turns his left foot 180° around to the left and places it one pace forwards in the direction of the throw.

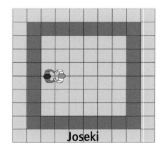

Joseki

Detail

Tori lets go of his grip on Uke's lapel and reaches through under Uke's left arm. He lays his flat hand on Uke's shoulder blade. In this variation of the grip, Tori pulls Uke continuously towards his body and at the same time upwards.

Detail

Tori places his stretched out leg a little forward and brings it in a sweeping movement forcibly to the rear.

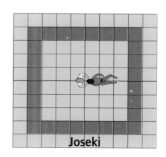

Tori moves his right leg forwards for the start of the throw and pulls Uke towards himself.

Uke is forced to move forward on his left foot towards Tori and is now standing parallel behind Tori.

Because Tori is increasing his pull, Uke loses his balance.

Uke is standing with his upper body upright and on the tips of his toes.

Uke tries to block the throw with his left hand on Tori's back but cannot prevent the throw.

Tori blocks Uke using the side of his hip and sweeps around forcibly with his outstretched right leg.

He bends forward and rotates his head and upper body at the same time to the left so that Uke is thrown with some force.

The turn of Tori's body is also very important here. Only when Tori turns his body to the left is he able to throw Uke forwards on to the Kata axis.

Uke falls down in front of Tori on the Kata axis. During the throw, Tori grasps hold of the arm of Uke's right sleeve with his right hand to ensure that Uke falls safely.

Joseki

▶▶▶ ▶▶▶ ▶▶▶

Tori and Uke stay for a short pause before they let go of their grip.

Uke lifts his upper body up. For this he bends his left knee up and supports himself on his left hand.

Uke stands up again coming up with his left knee and placing the right foot forward.

◀◀◀ ◀◀◀ ◀◀◀

◀◀◀ ◀◀◀ ◀◀◀

Tori and Uke arrive at the desired starting position for the next throw at the same time.

About 1 m in front of the red border of the mat, Uke turns around 180° to the left and moves to stand on the spot where the clothing is rearranged. Tori moves to a position just about an arm's length away from Uke.

Tori waits until Uke has stood up and then gets into step with him, walking behind him.

▶▶▶   ▶▶▶   ▶▶▶

Without pausing, he goes to the right side of the mat. Tori waits until Uke has stood up and in step with him, follows him.

About 1 m from the red border of the mat, Uke turns around 180°. Looking at Tori, he keeps his feet shoulder-width apart. Tori moves towards Uke until he is just about an arm's length from him.

Moving together, Tori and Uke move to the new starting position required.

Hidari-harai-goshi

◀◀◀   ◀◀◀   ◀◀◀

Transition to the right-sided Tsuri-komi-goshi

◀◀◀   ◀◀◀   ◀◀◀

Without pausing, he moves along the Kata axis to the left side of the mat.

Uke bends his right leg and brings his leg so that he is kneeling on his right knee. He then stands up easily.

Tori and Uke now have to move to the next starting position. After a short while they both let go of their grip.

1

The starting position for the Tsuri-komi-goshi is on the spot where the clothing is rearranged..

Detail

From the beginning, Tori grasps hold of the shoulder of Uke's jacket.

2

Uke launches his attack straight forward with his body upright.

From the beginning, Tori grasps hold of the left shoulder of Uke's jacket high up with his right hand. He maintains this grip up until the throw.

As normal, the left hand is holding the Judogi at elbow height.

At the same time as the grip, Uke takes the first sliding shuffle step towards Tori, who dodges backwards using the same appropriate footwork.

3

They now take the second sliding shuffle step.

It can be clearly seen here, that Tori exploits the pressure being applied by Uke and brings it over in the direction of the throw.

Without changing grip, Tori continues to pull with his left hand.

At the same time, Tori stretches his right arm and pulls Uke upwards a little. This brings Uke's upper body upright and slightly twisted.

4

On the next sliding shuffle step, Uke is brought forward off-balance.

For this, Tori pushes Uke right up with his right hand so that Uke almost has to stand on the tips of his toes.

The throw now begins. For this, as he moves backwards, Tori turns his left foot to the left in the direction of the throw.

He places his right foot next to Uke's right foot (his toes are pointing in the direction of the throw) and brings his left foot back in a circular motion to do the throw.

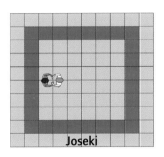

Joseki

Detail

Tori pushes Uke right up with the right hand of his stretched out arm. Uke is forced, therefore, to come into an upright posture.

Detail

Tori is standing parallel in front of Uke. Hip contact is made just underneath the center of Uke's balance. The hip should be twisted a little to the right.

5

6

7

After completing the third sliding shuffle step with his left foot towards Tori, Uke moves so that he is parallel behind his partner.

As a defense, Uke is supporting himself by leaning on Tori's back with his free left hand at about belt height. His fingers are pointing downwards.

Keeping hip contact, Tori slightly bends his knees. As he does this he pushes his hip a little to the right and thus comes underneath Uke's center of balance. Tori's right hand is pulling Uke right up. At the beginning of the throw and as he executes it, his right arm is outstretched.

Nevertheless, he keeps the pull on Uke's right arm well under control.

By stretching up from the legs and rotating his body a little to the left, coupled with a deliberate pulling of the arm, Tori throws Uke.

Uke is tipped with his body stretched out over Tori's hip. As in the other hip throwing techniques, the twist of the body (the head turns with the motion) is of great importance for its success when doing the Tsuri-komi-goshi.

Uke's body remains stretched out as he is thrown.

Uke falls down in front of Tori along the Kata axis.

Tori lets go with his right hand and reaches around Uke's right arm. As he does this he lifts his body upright.

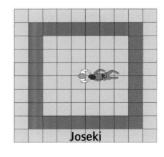

Joseki

▶▶▶ ▶▶▶ ▶▶▶

Tori and Uke stay for a short while in the Tsuri-komi-goshi end position and then let go of their grip.

As before, Uke stands up using his knee and leg.

He moves down the Kata axis to the right side of the mat. Tori waits until he has stood up and then follows him at a distance of about 1-2 m.

◀◀◀ ◀◀◀ ◀◀◀

◀◀◀ ◀◀◀ ◀◀◀

The length and speed of Tori's and Uke's steps are the same so that they arrive at the line running at right angles to the Kata axis at a spot about 0.5 m from the red border of the mat on the opposite side to the Joseki side at the same time.

For this, leading with his left foot, Tori moves diagonally to the left. At the same time, Uke also moves to the right at right angles to the Kata axis. However, as a mirror image, Uke leads off with his right foot.

They then turn together towards each other. The next throw takes place at right angles to the Kata axis. So that the throw can happen inside the red border of the mat, they form up outside the center of the mat.

▶▶▶

▶▶▶

▶▶▶

Tori gets into step with Uke so that they can be seen moving harmoniously.

About 1 m away from the red border of the mat, Uke turns 180° to the right and stands with his feet shoulder-width apart. Meanwhile, Tori takes a further step towards Uke.

Both reach their new starting position at the same time. They stand looking at each other at just about an arm's length apart.

Hidari-tsuri-komi-goshi

◀◀◀

◀◀◀

◀◀◀

Transition to the right-sided Okuri-ashi-barai

◀◀◀

◀◀◀

◀◀◀

Tori and Uke begin to count slowly to themselves first when they have reached the spot for rearrangement of their clothing. During this time, they have an opportunity to adjust their Judogi using deliberate, sharp hand movements.

For this, Uke stands up forward and moves directly to the left side of the mat. At the same time, Tori turns 180° around to the left and moves along the Kata axis to the right side of the mat. Both stand and keep looking outwards at a spot about 0.5 m inside the red border of the mat.

On completion of the Hidari-tsuri-komi-goshi, the second group – the Koshi-waza group of techniques – is ended and Uke and Tori let go of their grip and move to the position where the clothing is rearranged.

3rd Group:
Ashi-waza
(Leg and Foot Techniques)

- Okuri-ashi-barai
- Sasae-tsuri-komi-ashi
- Uchi-mata

Okuri-ashi-barai

Sasae-tsuri-komi-ashi

Uchi-mata

Okuri-ashi-barai

送
足
払

The preparatory steps and the Okuri-ashi-barai throw occur, exceptionally, at right angles to the Kata axis. Thus, the starting point is about 2.5 m away from the center of the mat on the Joseki side. Uke and Tori stand opposite each other just about an arm's length apart.

Detail

Tori's left hand grasps Uke's Judogi at the upper arm and presses it hard against the side of Uke's body so that the elbow is pressed towards his hip. As a result, Uke is forced to move sideways.

For a brief second, Uke intends to grab hold of Tori with a normal sleeve and collar grip. However, Tori is a fraction of a second quicker and attacks first.

Doing this, Tori forces his partner to move sideways by pressing his left hand hard against Uke's elbow.

Tori and Uke move sideways in the direction of the center of the mat with sliding shuffle steps, i.e. away from the Joseki side.

For this step, Tori places his right foot right out to the side and then brings his left foot up so that he is standing with feet shoulder-width apart.

As he does this he presses Uke's upper arm against the side of the body and the elbow towards the hips.

Uke is forced to move sideways by the force being applied. He moves his left foot first and pulls his right foot up until he is standing with feet shoulder-width apart.

Tori maintains the pressure he is exerting with his left hand throughout the throw.

The second step sideways is carried out in the same way but at an increased speed.

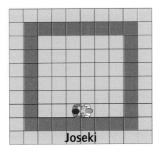

Joseki

Detail

On the third step sideways, Tori takes a much larger step forwards with his right foot a little towards Uke.

Detail

As he moves sideways, Uke's right foot is pushed onto his left foot and both feet are swept away in the direction of the movements. To do this, Tori places the sole of his foot outwards against Uke's ankle/outer side of the foot.

5

6

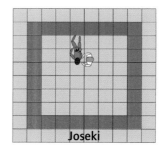

7

Both partners have brought their center of balance down by slightly bending their knees.

Care must be taken also that the shoulders always stay at the same height during the sideways steps.

On no account should a wavy or bumpy movement be visible.

On the third, larger step sideways, Tori moves his right foot a little forward towards Uke.

At the same time, Tori lifts Uke with both arms and pulls him upright. The sideways pressure, the lifting movement and the impetus from the sideways movement causes Uke to lose his balance.

To effect the throw, Tori places the sole of his left foot against Uke's right ankle/outer side of the foot and pushes Uke's right foot against his other left foot.

Combined with a forceful push from the left hand, Tori sweeps both of Uke's feet away together.

Tori throws his partner with the body upright but pushes his left hip right forward as he does the throw.

Tori steadies himself after the throw by taking a side step out to the right so that he comes to stand with feet shoulder-width apart behind Uke.

Tori grasps around Uke's arm with his right hand as he falls so that Uke lands under control and safely on his left-hand side.

Joseki

Uke falls down on the left side of his body in front of Tori. After pausing for a second Tori and Uke let go of their grip.

Tori remains standing upright looking directly forward. To stand up, Uke bends his left leg and supports himself on his left hand.

He brings his right foot up and then brings his left leg up into the standing position.

Tori and Uke are now standing opposite each other with feet shoulder-width apart. The distance between them is just about an arm's length.

About 1 m in front of the red border of the mat, Uke turns and stands on the Kata axis looking at the right-hand side of the mat. Meanwhile Tori moves towards Uke.

Uke moves down a line diagonal to the Kata axis to his own spot where the clothing is rearranged. Tori gets into step with him and they move together next to each other back to the Kata axis.

▶▶▶   ▶▶▶   ▶▶▶

As he stands upright, Uke turns to his left.

He moves towards Tori and ends up standing just about an arm's length in front of him.

Tori and Uke are standing opposite each other and they look at each other.

Hidari-okuri-ashi-barai

◀◀◀   ◀◀◀   ◀◀◀

Transition to the right-sided Sasae-tsuri-komi-ashi

◀◀◀   ◀◀◀   ◀◀◀

He turns straight away a little to the right in the required direction and ends standing up. At the same time, Tori takes a small step forwards with his left foot so that he is standing level next to Uke.

To stand up, Uke bends his right knee and pushes his left foot out.

After a short pause in the end position, Tori and Uke let go of their grip.

支
釣
込
足

Starting position for the Sasae-tsuri-komi-ashi: Uke is standing about 1m inside the red border of the mat with Tori opposite him at about arm's length away. After a short pause, Uke attacks.

Detail

Tori uses his weight by leaning backwards without losing his balance. The pull on the arm is kept forwards in the direction of the throw.

Uke moves to grasp Tori and takes a sliding shuffle step (Tsugi-ashi) towards him. The attack is done with a straight back. Uke is exerting pressure forwards against Tori's shoulders parallel to the mat.

Tori also grasps hold of Uke and dodges back with the appropriate footwork to the rear – left foot is placed to the rear and the right foot is brought back to it.

Uke now does the second sliding shuffle step. Accordingly, Tori takes a normal pace backwards with his left foot.

Uke keeps up the pressure on Tori's shoulders right up to the actual throw.

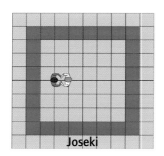

Tori, however, does not bring the right foot alongside his left as usual, but halts the rhythm of the attack as he takes his second step.

Tori brings his right foot around in a semi-circle past his left foot and places it down on the mat at right angles to the direction of the movement to the right of the Kata axis. The tips of the toes are pointing at the Joseki side.

As a result, Tori dodges a little around Uke. Tori keeps pulling forward on Uke's arm in the direction of the throw.

The correct positioning of the right foot – as described above – is very important.

Joseki

Detail

Tori dodges around to the side as he takes the second step. For this he turns his right foot 90° to the right. This is important, because during the throw, Tori has to turn his right foot around a further 90° in order to get into the end position.

Detail

Tori stops Uke's leg moving forward – that is weighed down by Uke's body – by placing the sole of his foot down on it at about the height of the ankle joint.

5

6

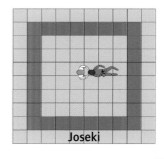

7

Tori pulls forcibly forwards and forces Uke to take a third sliding shuffle step.

Tori uses his body weight for the throw. He leans over backwards without losing his balance.

Tori has placed the center of his body weight over his right foot and thus, he can carry out the Sasae-tsuri-komi-ashi throw.

He does this by placing the sole of his left foot down on the ankle joint of Uke's right foot just at the moment that Uke has placed his weight on the right foot as he comes forward and is about to pull the left foot up to it.

Tori's forcible pull on the arm, combined with his back leaning to the rear, clearly causes Uke to lose his balance.

As mentioned already, due to Tori dodging slightly to the side, Uke falls over the leg that has been placed down on his foot.

Tori checks the throw by following through with Uke's movements. He turns his body further to the left on the foot that is already turned sideways to the right. He then places his left foot down shoulder-width away from his right foot.

Uke lands, displaced a little to the left, parallel to the Kata axis.

Joseki

71

▶▶▶   ▶▶▶   ▶▶▶

Tori and Uke pause for a short while in the end position and then let go of their grip.

To stand up, Uke bends his left leg up and supports himself on his left hand.

He places his right foot forward and stands by bringing his left leg up.

◀◀◀   ◀◀◀   ◀◀◀

◀◀◀   ◀◀◀   ◀◀◀

Looking from Joseki, Tori is standing on the right-hand side and Uke is on the left. The distance between them is about 1.5 m.

Uke adjusts his position so that he also comes to stand on the Kata axis just about 1 m away from the center of the mat.

When standing upright, Uke turns around to the left. His right foot is placed in the direction of Tori. Uke finally stands upright.

▶▶▶   ▶▶▶   ▶▶▶

Without pausing, Uke moves along the Kata axis to the right side of the mat. Tori follows him in step.	About 1 m from the right-hand mat border, Uke turns around 180° to the right. He stands looking at the center of the mat.	At the same time, Tori – like Uke – reaches the new starting position and is standing just about one arm's length away from Uke.

Hidari-sasae-tsuri-komi-ashi

◀◀◀   ◀◀◀   ◀◀◀

Transition to the right-sided Uchi-mata

◀◀◀   ◀◀◀   ◀◀◀

Tori is now standing on the Kata axis about 1m away from the center of the mat. Then Uke bends his left leg, kneels on it and brings right knee up.	While Uke is standing up, Tori adjusts his position. Usually he only has to take a step backwards so that he is in the required starting position.	After a short pause, Tori and Uke let go of their grip.

Uchi-mata

内
股

For the starting position of the Uchi-mata, Tori and Uke meet in the center of the mat. They are about 1.5 m away from each other. Both pause for a second in this position.

Detail

In a normal sleeve and collar grip, the elbows are lifted up to shoulder height. When both Tori and Uke pull slightly against each other, the arms come into a rounded, tense position.

Tori and Uke move towards each other, leading with the right foot and at the same time attack.

Both use the normal sleeve and collar grip, i.e. the left hand grasps the Judogi underneath the partner's right elbow while the right hand grasps the collar at collarbone height.

The elbows are lifted up to shoulder height to achieve the rounded-arm position. Tori and Uke both pull a little outwards so the arms are tensed without them losing their balance.

Uchi-mata is performed from a circular motion. Tori takes the initiative and, leading with the left foot, swings it around in a semi-circular motion outwards past Uke's right foot that is placed forwards.

Coupled with a forceful tug with the right arm on Uke's lapel, Tori follows this up by moving his right foot to a shoulder-width, firm stand.

Correspondingly to the tug of the arm, first of all Uke has to follow Tori's circular leg motion. Uke brings his right foot up and is now standing in a slightly larger than shoulder-width position opposite Tori.

Tori's rounded grip and constant tugging causes Uke to lean forward so that he cannot stand on the flat of his feet but rather more on the tips of his toes.

The second step is done similarly.

Tori leads with his left foot and swings it in a semi-circular motion outwards past Uke. Coupled with the tug on the arm, Tori pulls his right foot around and Uke has to follow firstly Tori's pull and movements with his left foot and then with his right foot.

Both move along in a circular motion at a circumference of about 1 m depending on Tori's and Uke's size.

The circular motion takes place in the center of the mat.

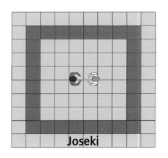

Joseki

Detail

Sequence of steps for the circular motion.

On the third step, the circular motion is continued with Tori's left foot placed a little forward.

As he does this, the toes of his foot point to the right corner of the mat on the Joseki side.

Accordingly, Uke has to follow around Tori first with his left foot and then back with his right foot.

To execute the throw, Tori pulls Uke forward in the direction of the foot of his standing leg and causes Uke to lose his balance.

Tori sweeps his right leg hard up backwards so that it strikes against the center of Uke's left thigh and Uke is thrown with an Ashi-uchi-mata.

As he throws Uke, Tori bends his upper body right forward and turns it slightly to the left at the same time.

Tori stands firmly upright in the end position behind Uke. He grasps Uke's right arm with his right arm to assist Uke in the fall.

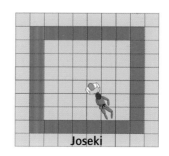

Joseki

After a successful throw and a short pause, Tori and Uke let go of their grip.

Tori will be able to reach the new starting position by taking three steps backwards (left, right, left). He is now standing on the Kata axis just about 1 m away from the center of the mat.

In the meantime, Uke stands up from his left knee with his right foot placed – knee up – forward.

For the new starting position, Tori and Uke are now standing in the center of the mat about 1.5 m apart.

Tori and Uke take four paces towards each other. Both lead with their left feet.

When the count is ended, both turn towards each other at the same time – Tori around to his right and Uke to his left.

▶▶▶ ▶▶▶ ▶▶▶

Without pausing, he goes back to the Kata axis.

Uke also stands about 1 m away from the center of the mat.

Tori and Uke are standing on the Kata axis – Tori is on the left-hand half of the mat with Uke on the right-hand half. They are standing about 1.5 m apart.

Hidari-uchi-mata

◀◀◀ ◀◀◀ ◀◀◀

Transition to the right-sided Tomoe-nage

◀◀◀ ◀◀◀ ◀◀◀

Looking outwards, both begin to count together to themselves. While they do this they both have an opportunity to adjust their clothing.

Uke has already stood up so that he can go to the left side of the mat. Without pausing, Tori and Uke move to the spot where they can adjust their clothing.

After completing the Hidari-uchi-mata, this concludes the Ashi-waza grouping techniques. While Tori turns around to the left to the right-hand side of the mat, Uke stands up from his right knee.

4th Group:
Ma-sutemi-waza
('Sacrificial Throws on the Back' Techniques)

- Tomoe-nage
- Ura-nage
- Sumi-gaeshi

Tomoe-nage

Ura-nage

Sumi-gaeshi

Starting position for the Tomoe-nage: Tori and Uke meet in the center of the mat about 1.5 m apart from each other. They pause and look at each other.

Leading with the right foot and taking a pace towards each other, both attack at the same time.

They are now standing in the center of the mat using the normal grip on each other and the normal footwork. Both try to force the other backwards. They tussle to achieve this. Tori then manages to force Uke back by applying increased pressure forwards. For this Tori pushes Uke and at the same time takes a short step towards Uke again with the right foot.

Confronted with the strong push by Tori, Uke has to take a small step to dodge backwards with his left foot.

Tori is still moving forwards applying pressure on Uke thus forcing him to take the next two steps also backwards before Uke can establish a firm standing position.

First of all, Tori moves his left foot towards Uke who then takes a step back with his right foot.

It is not until he has taken the third step that Uke is in a position to stop Tori.

While Tori moves forward with his right foot, Uke places his left foot back and lowers his center of balance, blocking Tori from his hip.

Tori exploits Uke's action (in a competition called an 'edge of the mat situation') in order to throw Uke with a Tomoe-nage.

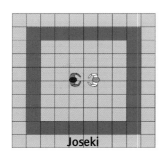

Joseki

真
捨
身
技

Detail

To change over his grip, Tori lets go of the sleeve of the jacket with his left hand and reaches through underneath Uke's right arm to take hold of his right lapel.

Detail

Tori uses the weight of his body by leaning his upper body backwards. This way, he has room to bring his right foot up and place it on Uke's middle, around belt height.

5

6

7

Tori now reaches around with his left hand (see 'Detail') and at the same time brings his left foot one pace towards Uke and places it down next to his own right foot underneath Uke's center of balance. Tori stretches up and pulls Uke up using both hands on the Judogi. Tori already starts to let himself fall backwards using the whole of his bodyweight to cause Uke to come forward off-balance. Because of the pull, Uke has to bring his left leg from the rear forward. His feet are now together and his center of balance is forward and no longer under control. Tori lets himself fall forcibly rearwards in order to throw Uke and places his right foot up into Uke's middle at around belt height.

The action of Tori's body falling backwards causes Uke to take a pace forwards and eventually fall over.

In the throw, Tori stretches his right leg in the direction of the throw and pulls Uke with both hands in a collar grip over his head in a wide arc. Uke lets go of his grip on the lapel and turns the flat of his hand outwards so that his elbows are pointing in the direction of the throw.

He falls straight over Tori down the line of the Kata axis and up into a firm standing position.

In the end position one can see that Tori's left leg is stretched up and his bottom is raised up off the ground. Tori follows through the throw on Uke with his arms and these are brought back to his sides at chest height before he stands up.

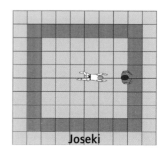

Joseki

▶▶▶   ▶▶▶   ▶▶▶

Tori and Uke pause for a second in the end position.	Tori bends his left leg up to stand up and supports himself on his left hand. At the same time Uke turns around 180° to his left.	Uke moves along the Kata axis in the direction the center of the mat. Tori stands up bringing his left knee up and placing his right foot on the ground.

◀◀◀   ◀◀◀   ◀◀◀

◀◀◀   ◀◀◀   ◀◀◀

Having arrived at the center of the mat Tori stands still. Tori and Uke are about 2 m apart.	Tori moves along the Kata axis towards Uke. Uke is already standing on the Kata axis with his feet shoulder-width apart about 1 m inside the red border of the mat.	While he turns, Tori also turns 180° but around to the right.

▶▶▶   ▶▶▶   ▶▶▶

Tori now turns around 180° to the left while Uke continues on without a pause.

Tori and Uke move towards each other along the Kata axis.

At the center of the mat they stand about 1.5 m apart from each other. As seen from the Joseki side, Uke is standing on the right-hand side and Tori on the left.

Hidari-tomoe-nage

◀◀◀   ◀◀◀   ◀◀◀

Transition to the right-sided Ura-nage

◀◀◀   ◀◀◀   ◀◀◀

For this he brings his left foot and his right knee up. Uke turns around 180° to his left – slowly and almost on the spot.

Tori now bends his right leg up and stands up.

After the Hidari-tomoe-nage throw has been completed, Tori and Uke remain in the end position for a short pause.

Ura-nage

蓑
投

In the starting position for the Ura-nage, Tori and Uke are standing about 2 m apart on the Kata axis. Tori is in the center of the mat.

Uke takes a step forwards and at the same time pulls his bunched right fist back for a punch.

He holds his left fist, also bunched, in front of his body as a defense.

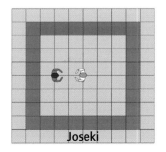

With his next step, Uke moves his right foot forward targeting Tori.

As he does this he brings his right fist right up and completes the punch on Tori's head bringing his fist downwards.

The attack resembles driving a post into the ground – his body is leaning forwards. Tori has to react quickly.

He moves towards Uke, taking two quick paces forwards – first with the right foot and then the left.

By bending his knees, Tori ducks down underneath the punching arm.

As he does this he reaches further around behind Uke's back with his left arm at belt height.

Tori lays the flat of his right hand on the front of Uke's stomach at about the height of the knot of the belt.

The fingers of the hand are pointing upwards. Tori pulls Uke really close to his body so that the right-hand side of Uke's chest is in close contact with his own upper body. The left-hand side of Tori's head is lying on Uke's chest.

Detail

Tori lays the flat of his right hand on Uke's stomach at about the height of the knot of the belt. The fingers of the hand are pointing upwards.

Joseki

真
捨
身
技

Detail

Tori's left hand grasps right around Uke's hip by bringing his arm along the line of Uke's belt.

Detail

Tori pulls Uke really close to his body and establishes a close contact between the left-hand side of his own left shoulder/head and the right-hand side of Uke's body.

5

Tori now pushes his hips right forward and stretches over backwards and lets himself fall down onto the area of his upper back/shoulders. At the same time he pushes Uke hard, right up in the air, by pulling with his left hand and applying pressure with the flat of his right hand.

Uke is thrown over Tori's left shoulder. Tori keeps his hips up throughout the throw. He pushes the balls of his feet – not his heels – firmly down into the mat.

6

Uke's attack and forwards movement must not become slowed down or blocked, rather they must be picked up and moved on.

Tori must show he has control over Uke as he throws him and watches out that the body contact with Uke is not lost as he executes the throw.

Uke falls down freely over Tori. As he falls, he brings his right arm in to his body so that it doesn't get jammed under Tori's back.

7

Uke lands on the Kata axis. Tori's arms follow through in the direction of the throw. His bottom is held up and the balls of his feet are firmly pressed into the mat.

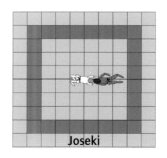

Joseki

▶▶▶   ▶▶▶   ▶▶▶

After pausing for a short while in the Ura-nage end position, Tori and Uke stand up.	First of all, both bend their left legs and push themselves up.	They then stand up, bringing their left knees up and placing their right feet on the ground.

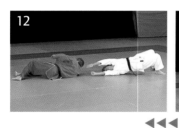

◀◀◀   ◀◀◀   ◀◀◀

◀◀◀   ◀◀◀   ◀◀◀

Seen from the Joseki side, Uke is standing on the left just about 1 m away from the red border of the mat. Tori is standing about 1 m away from him.	While Uke has reached the required position when turning around, Tori has to take a few steps to move towards Uke.	They are standing on the Kata axis looking at each other.

▶▶▶

▶▶▶

▶▶▶

So that they don't turn their backs on the Joseki side, Tori turns around to the left and Uke to the right. Both stand looking at each other on the Kata axis.

After turning around, Uke ends up about 1 m away from the red border of the mat. Meanwhile, Tori moves to the center of the mat, i.e. towards Uke.

Tori and Uke stand opposite each other about 2 m apart.

Hidari-ura-nage

◀◀◀

◀◀◀

◀◀◀

Transition to the right-sided Sumi-gaeshi

◀◀◀

◀◀◀

◀◀◀

Tori and Uke stand and turn around 180° towards each other – Tori around to the right and Uke to the left.

To stand up both bend their right leg up. They kneel on their right knee and place their left foot forward.

Tori and Uke remain a second in the end position and then stand up together.

Sumi-gaeshi

隅返

For the starting position in the Sumi-gaeshi, Uke stands at the edge of the left-hand mat border on the spot where the clothing may be rearranged. Tori stands opposite him about 1 m away.

Detail

The defensive posture (Migi-jigotai) is adopted by Uke standing on the spot for rearrangement of the clothing from the first step. In this stance, the knees are bent and turned slightly outwards. Uke and Tori are standing parallel with each other. Their knees and toes of their feet are almost touching.

Both move towards each other with the right foot and both attack at the same time.

The position of the feet and hands are identical (see 'Detail'). Both have dropped the center of their balance lower in this broad positioning of the feet. Tori's and Uke's upper bodies are upright and they lean a little to the rear in order to get their partner to come forward off balance. The tension is maintained by taking a firm, sure grip.

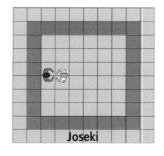

Joseki

The following second step is done in a circular motion.

Tori's hard pull with his right hand and the simultaneous, circular motion of setting his right foot back forces Uke to move forward towards Tori with his left foot.

The defensive posture, with feet wide apart, is maintained.

The tension held by them both with their grip – described already above – is kept up by both of them leaning their upper bodies back and maintaining the pull on each with a firm grip.

With his third step, Tori places his left foot straight back one side to the left of the Kata axis at about the height of his right foot.

By pulling on Uke's upper arm and with a circular, right-footed movement, Tori forces Uke to come forward.

Tori stretches up and moves the weight of his body to the rear.

Tori's legs are stretched out. Uke tries to defend himself against Tori's increasing pull by moving the weight of his body a little to the rear and thus keeping the tension between them.

Detail

The right hand is pushed through under the armpit and is lying on the shoulder blade. The left hand grasps hold of the upper arm (not the Judogi). By bending the arms and lifting the elbows up to shoulder height you achieve a rounded grip with the arms. Tori and Uke use the same grip.

Detail

To do the throw, Tori places the instep of the right foot on the inside against Uke's thigh.

Detail

Uke lets go with his right hand and turns his elbow so that it is pointing in the direction of the throw. When falling, he rolls from his lower arm over Tori's upper arm. The arm is not taken out from the armpit.

5

To do the throw, Tori lies right back and uses the whole of the weight of his body.

At the same time, he pulls Uke towards him so that Uke quite clearly will lose his balance. Uke reacts to Tori's attack by taking a large step with his right foot in the direction of the throw.

Because Tori continually pulls on Uke's upper body, despite Uke's dodging movement, he is successful in coming underneath Uke's center of balance.

Tori places the instep of his right foot on the inside of Uke's left thigh and pushes Uke with this in the direction of the throw.

6

Uke can now not offer any further resistance and falls over forwards over Tori with a big Judo forward roll.

As he does this, he lets go of the grip with his right hand and turns his wrist over clockwise so that his elbow is pointing in the direction of the throw.

His hand is not pulled out from underneath Tori's armpit – thus Uke rolls away over the upper arm with his right arm.

Uke ends up on the Kata axis around about the spot where the rearrangement of Tori's clothing occurs. He stands with his feet firmly placed shoulder-width apart.

7

Tori's arms follow through in the direction of the throw. His left foot is kept firmly on the mat with his hips lifted up and the right foot still in the air.

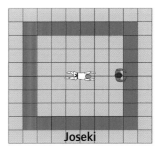

Joseki

▶▶▶   ▶▶▶   ▶▶▶

The Sumi-gaeshi end position.

After a short pause, Tori stands up. He bends his left leg up and places his right foot out.

Tori stands up bringing his left knee up.

◀◀◀   ◀◀◀   ◀◀◀

◀◀◀   ◀◀◀   ◀◀◀

He keeps just about an arm's length away from Uke.

Uke remains standing on this position after turning. Leading with his left foot, Tori moves along the Kata axis towards Uke.

They then both turn at the same time towards each other. Tori turns around to the right and Uke to the left.

▶▶▶   ▶▶▶   ▶▶▶

He then turns around to the left. Tori is standing roughly in the center of the mat looking at its right-hand side.

While Tori moves towards Uke along the Kata axis, Uke turns around 180° to the right.

Uke stops on the spot where Tori rearranges his clothing. Tori moves to reach a position about 1 m away from Uke. They are now standing opposite each other with feet shoulder-width apart.

Hidari-sumi-gaeshi

◀◀◀   ◀◀◀   ◀◀◀

Transition to the right-sided Yoko-gake

◀◀◀   ◀◀◀   ◀◀◀

Both now begin to count to themselves and rearrange their Judo clothing.

Tori moves along the Kata axis to the right-hand side of the mat to the spot where the rearrangement of the clothing takes place. Uke is usually already in the correct position and waits until Tori has reached his.

The completion of the Hidari-sumi-gaeshi concludes Kata of the Fourth Group. Tori stands up by bringing up his bent right leg.

5ᵗʰ Group:
Yoko-sutemi-waza
('Sacrificial Throws on the Side' Techniques)

▌ Yoko-gake
▌ Yoko-guruma
▌ Uki-waza

Yoko-gake

Yoko-guruma

Uki-waza

Starting position for the Yoko-gake: Uke is standing on the spot where clothing can be rearranged. Tori is standing opposite just about an arm's length away from him. Both pause for a second.

Uke attacks first and takes a sliding shuffle step (right foot is moved forwards with the left feet then pulled up) towards Tori.

The pressure of the attack is directed forwards towards Tori's shoulders.

Uke is standing upright as he does this. Tori also attacks and dodges back similarly to the rear (left foot moves back followed by pulling the right back).

During the following, second sliding shuffle steps, Tori takes up and uses the movements of Uke's attack.

For this Tori turns Uke's upper body slightly to the side by pushing Uke's elbow from the outside with his left hand and at the same time pushing Uke's left shoulder to the rear with his right hand.

Uke is therefore forced to place more of his weight over his right foot. As with the first step taken, Tori and Uke move along the Kata axis as they carry out the steps.

On the third step, Tori increases the pressure on Uke's elbows. Uke's upper body still remains in an upright position. Just as in the Okuri-ashi-barai, Uke is lifted upwards off balance.

He is now standing a little askew to the Kata axis. Tori's aim is to get Uke in an upright body position to be balanced on the front of his right foot, i.e. on the smallest possible area.

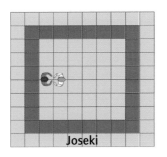

Joseki

Detail

Tori's strong, hard pull forward and upwards with both hands forces Uke to place his body weight onto the front of his right foot and so become off-balance because he is not standing on a larger area.

Detail

The sole of Tori's left foot is pressing firmly from the outside onto Uke's ankle. Uke's left leg lies against his own right foot, without touching the mat. During the execution of the throw, Uke's stretched body is slightly leaning in the direction of the throw.

5

6

7

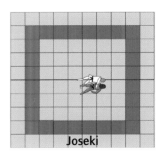

Tori pulls Uke up and towards him with both hands. Uke's left leg follows this movement and is no longer placed down on the mat. Uke is off-balance in this position. To start the throw, Tori takes a short step with his right foot towards Uke without allowing Uke's situation and position to change. He quickly places the sole of his left foot on the outside of Uke's right ankle and presses hard and firmly against it so that Uke's right foot is swept away from underneath his body.

Uke's left leg remains parallel to his right leg without contact with the mat and during the throw is not placed down again.

At the same time, Tori pulls his partner to him with his left hand and pushes him away with his right hand. This way, Uke is turned onto the left side of his body during the fall and lands safely.

Tori also throws himself onto the left side of his body and accompanies Uke down to the ground. As this happens, the sole of Tori's left foot remains constantly in contact with Uke's ankle – similarly, contact is maintained with the grip on Uke's Judogi and arm.

Tori and Uke land on the Kata axis. The feet are towards the center of the mat.

If the throw is correctly executed, Uke falls fairly hard.

Joseki

▶▶▶ ▶▶▶ ▶▶▶

Tori and Uke remain for a short while in the end position and then let go of their grip.

To stand up they first of all bend the left leg up and support themselves on the their left hand.

They both kneel up at the same time. To do this they turn a little to the left and place the right foot up.

◀◀◀ ◀◀◀ ◀◀◀

◀◀◀ ◀◀◀ ◀◀◀

Tori and Uke are standing about 2 m opposite each other.

As he gets to the center of the mat, Tori stands with his feet shoulder-width apart. Uke continues on until he reaches and turns around, 180° to his right, at a spot about 1m inside the red border of the mat standing on the Kata axis.

Both move, in step, straight forward. Tori is on the Kata axis and Uke is to the left of him.

▶▶▶   ▶▶▶   ▶▶▶

Having stood up, they turn a little further to the left so that they are alongside each other looking at the right-hand side of the mat. Without a pause and moving together, both carry on straight forward.

Tori moves along the Kata axis and Uke alongside him on the right, taking somewhat larger steps. Just about 1 m away from the red border of the mat, Uke turns around 180° to his left.

He adjusts his position so that he is on the Kata axis and looking at Tori, who continues to stand in a position just about an arm's length away from Uke. In an ideal situation, both arrive at the new starting position at the same time.

Hidari-yoko-gake

◀◀◀   ◀◀◀   ◀◀◀

Transition to the right-sided Yoko-guruma

◀◀◀   ◀◀◀   ◀◀◀

Having stood up from their left foot, both turn around a little further to the right so that they have now completed a 180° movement and are standing looking at the left-hand side of the mat alongside each other.

They both stand up together. Both kneel on their left knee with their right foot placed out. As they do this they twist a little to the right.

On completion of the Hidari-yoko-gake, both bend their right legs up and support themselves on their right hand.

Yoko-guruma

横車

For the starting position of the Yoko-guruma, Tori is standing in the center of the mat. Uke is on the left-hand side of the mat about 2 m away from him. They stand like this opposite each other for a short while.

Detail

Tori's firm grip with his left hand reaches right around Uke's hip. The flat of his right hand is pushing against the front of Uke's stomach at about belt height (the fingers are pointing upwards).

Uke then attacks with a right-fisted punch.

To do this, similar to the Ura-nage, Uke first of all takes a step forward with his left foot towards Tori and pulls his right clenched fist back.

He holds his clenched left fist in front of his body.

In order to execute the punch attack, Uke now takes a second step.

He takes a step directly towards Tori with his right foot. Uke brings his right fist from way back and brings it over forward in a wide arc to strike down onto Tori's head.

With the aim of executing a Ura-nage throw, Tori takes two rapid steps towards Uke. This he does by, first of all, taking a step forward with his right foot and then a step to the outside past the right-hand side of Uke's body with his left foot.

He ends up, with his knees slightly bent, in front of and quite close underneath Uke's center of balance.

Tori ducks underneath Uke's attacking arm and grasps along Uke's belt, right around his hips with his left hand.

At the same time, Tori lays the flat of his right hand (fingers pointing upwards) on the front of Uke's stomach.

Uke recognizes Tori's intention and prevents the repeat of a Ura-nage by bending his upper body slightly forward and at the same time dropping his hips lower. Doing this, he lowers his center of balance further downwards.

Because of Uke's reaction, Tori is also drawn downwards by Uke's attacking arm.

Joseki

Detail

To prevent an Ura-nage being executed, Uke drops his hips and thus brings his center of balance lower. He is now standing firmly with his upper body leaning slightly forwards. The lift and the throw for an Ura-nage is almost impossible from this position.

Detail

Tori places his right foot firmly on the mat between Uke's legs. He lets himself fall backwards and uses all of his body weight in doing so. Uke is also rotated in the throw by Tori's firm pull and the close contact between their hips.

5

Tori maintains the firm grip on Uke's hips, but dodges Uke's pressing and adjusts his center of balance.

To do this, he places his right foot in a semi-circular motion from the front between Uke's legs. Tori lets himself fall backwards using his body weight.

As he does this, both of his feet remain firmly on the mat. Uke reacts by also bringing his center of balance to the rear so that there is an impasse – like in the Sumi-gaeshi – in strength between Tori and Uke. Tori brings Uke off balance by making a firm pull on Uke's hips with his left hand. At the same time, he leans further backwards and pushes Uke up with his right hand in the direction of the throw.

6

Uke goes over with his body rotating onto the ground. For the execution of the throw, Tori pushes his hips up as he falls in order to achieve the necessary tension. His bottom doesn't touch the mat.

With this Yoko-guruma, Uke is thrown with great force over Tori's left shoulder. So that he can easily do a forward roll, Uke brings his right arm right forwards.

He falls, in the direction he is going, onto the left-hand side of the mat, i.e. on the opposite side to Joseki.

7

Uke comes up to stand firmly with feet shoulder-width apart. Tori's bottom is still off the mat and his arms follow through in the direction of the throw. Tori looks over backwards towards his partner.

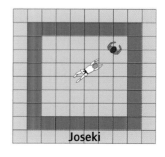

Joseki

Tori and Uke pause for a second in the end position.

While Tori bends his left leg up, Uke begins to turn around to the right.

Tori turns around to the left as he stands up until he is able to place his right foot up and forward on the Kata axis. Tori is kneeling on his left knee and is looking at the right-hand side of the mat.

Tori and Uke are now standing in the position required for the start of the Uki-waza.

Having reached the Kata axis, Uke turns around 90° to the left and is now standing in the required position, looking at Tori. At the same time, Tori comes to stand about 1 m away from Uke.

While Tori moves along the Kata axis to the left-hand side of the mat, Uke moves towards the Joseki side until he reaches the spot where clothing is rearranged.

▶▶▶　　　　　　　　　　　　▶▶▶　　　　　　　　　　　　▶▶▶

While Tori finishes standing up, Uke moves directly in the direction of the Kata axis along a line parallel to the red border of the mat.

Tori moves to the center of the mat and remains standing there. At the same time, having arrived at the Kata axis, Uke turns 90° around to the left.

The aim is that Tori and Uke arrive at the starting position both at the same time and are standing about 2 m opposite each other in the right half of the mat, ready for the Hidari-yoko-guruma.

Hidari-yoko-guruma

◀◀◀　　　　　　　　　　　　◀◀◀　　　　　　　　　　　　◀◀◀

Transition to the right-sided Uki-waza

Both take a pace towards each other with the right foot and attack simultaneously.

The position of Tori's and Uke's feet and hands are identical (see 'Detail' photos). Both have adopted a wide positioning of the feet and the center of balance of their bodies is lowered.

The upper bodies remain upright and the center of balance is leaning slightly to the rear.

Starting position for the Uki-waza: Uke is standing on the left-hand edge of the mat on the spot where clothing is rearranged. Tori is standing about 1 m away opposite him.

The following second step is done in a circular motion.

Tori pulls Uke firmly with the right hand towards himself and brings his right foot back in a circular motion.

This forces Uke to have to bring his left foot also in a circular motion towards Tori. The defensive posture with feet slightly

Detail

The defensive posture is adopted already during the first step. For this, the feet are well apart and the knees bent and turned slightly outwards. Uke and Tori are standing parallel to each other with their knees and the tips of their toes almost touching.

Without pausing, Tori moves his left foot to the rear. He brings his foot up alongside his right foot without placing it down on the mat.

Uke recognizes the situation and the danger that he can be caught with a Sumi-gaeshi

横
捨
身
技

Detail

The right hand is pushed through under the armpit and is lying on the shoulder blade. The left hand is grasping the upper arm (not the Judogi). A rounded arm position is achieved by bending the arms and lifting the elbows. Tori and Uke are gripping each other in the same manner.

Detail

Uke lets go of his grip with the right hand and turns the arm so that the elbow is pointing in the direction of the throw. As he falls, he rolls over Tori's upper arm with his lower arm. The arm is not taken out from underneath the armpit.

5

Tori reacts to Uke's movements and alters the direction of the throw.

Again, Tori uses the whole weight of his body to execute the Uki-waza. While Uke places his right foot forward, Tori stretches his left leg right out without placing the foot on the mat. At the same time, Tori pulls Uke's right upper arm with his left hand in the direction of the right-hand corner of the mat (as seen from Uke's position). Tori's right arm supports this movement by applying corresponding pressure under Uke's armpit.

6

Tori's left leg acts as an additional element of the impetus in this way. It should, as far as possible, follow through in the direction of the throw and only then at the end be placed down on the mat.

Uke twists his right hand outwards and to soften the fall brings the arm right forward.

He does a Judo roll forward and comes up to stand firmly, feet shoulder-width apart, in the right-hand corner of the mat (i.e., towards Joseki).

7

Both of Tori's feet are firmly pressed down onto the ground and his bottom is lifted up from the mat. He keeps his eyes on Uke throughout the throw and his arms follow through in the direction of the throw.

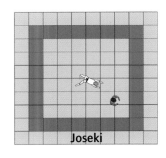

Joseki

▶▶▶ ▶▶▶ ▶▶▶

Tori and Uke pause for a second in the Uki-waza end position.

While Uke moves straight ahead, Tori starts to stand up by bending his left leg and supporting himself on his left hand.

Tori stands up bringing his left knee up and placing his right foot forward to the ground.

◀◀◀ ◀◀◀ ◀◀◀

◀◀◀ ◀◀◀ ◀◀◀

Tori and Uke use the pause to adjust their Judoki. Then, simultaneously, they turn towards each other. Tori turns to his right and Uke to his left. Both are now standing, feet shoulder-width apart, opposite each other.

Having arrived at the Kata axis, he turns around 90° to the left and stands still. At the same time, Tori also reaches his position. Both are standing just about 1m inside the red border of the mat looking outwards.

While Tori moves along the Kata axis to his position on the spot where clothing is rearranged, Uke takes the direct route to his own position for adjusting the clothing on the left-hand side of the mat.

▶▶▶ ▶▶▶ ▶▶▶

Tori turns around about 180° to the left so that he is standing on the Kata axis, looking at the right-hand side of the mat. Uke turns to the left and, exceptionally, when he takes the next step his back is pointing at the Joseki side.

Tori moves along the Kata axis, Uke parallel to the red border of the mat. Having arrived at the Kata axis, Uke turns around 90° to the left and stands in the required position looking at Tori. At the same time, Tori comes to within 1m from Uke.

Tori and Uke are now standing in the new starting position for the Hidari-uki-waza.

Hidari-uki-waza

◀◀◀ ◀◀◀ ◀◀◀

Transition to the final greeting

◀◀◀ ◀◀◀ ◀◀◀

Tori stands up bringing his right knee up and placing his left foot on the ground. At the same time, Uke turns around 90° to the right and moves off straight ahead with his back pointing towards the Joseki side.

He bends his right leg up and brings his upper body upwards.

After the Hidari-uki-waza throw has been completed, this concludes the fifth and last element of the Nage-no-Kata. Tori and Uke pause shortly in the end position and then Tori starts to stand up.

The Final Greeting

After the last rearrangement of their clothing, Tori and Uke turn towards each other and stand about 0.5m inside the red border of the mat. **(Photo 1)**

Both partners place, first of all, their right foot and then their left foot back, changing over from the feet at shoulder-width distance apart to one where the feet are close together. **(Photo 2)**

The heels are almost touching each other while the feet form an angle of about 60°. At the end of the demonstration, the sequence of the final greeting takes place now in the reverse order to the starting greeting. **(Photo 3)**

▶▶▶

First of all, Tori and Uke kneel down for the bow towards each other. To do this they place their left leg, propped up on the toes, to the rear so that their kneeling left knee is level with their right foot on the surface of the mat. **(Photo 4)**

Straight away, they bring their right knee parallel into the kneeling position. The toes of the feet are propped up. **(Photo 5)**

Tori and Uke sit down on the heels/lower legs. Their toes are moved so that both feet are lying parallel to each other. At the same time, as done in the starting greeting, Tori and Uke take hold of the ends of their belts and lay them right and left to the sides. Afterwards, the hands are brought back and laid on the thighs. **(Photo 6)**

►►►

After a short pause, both partners bow towards each other. For this the hands on the thighs glide downwards to the surface of the mat. The thumbs are stretched out so that the hands form a triangle about 10 cm from each other. They keep looking at their hands and their bottoms are not lifted off their heels. **(Photo 7)**

After Tori and Uke have lifted their bodies back up, both come back into a kneeling position with their toes flattened out. **(Photo 8)**

To stand up, first of all they bring the right foot up and then the left one. **(Photo 9)**

▶▶▶

Tori and Uke now stand with their feet close together and bodies upright. The arms are hanging loosely down by their sides. **(Photo 10)**

After a short moment, both turn towards the Joseki side – Tori to the left and Uke to the right. **(Photo 11)**

They now bow together towards the Joseki. The hands glide from the sides of the body onto the front of the thighs and downwards in the direction of the knees. The head follows the movements of the body so that for a moment they are looking downwards at the mat. Tori and Uke bring their bodies back up and retreat backwards away off the mat. **(Photo 12)**

Appendices
Concluding Remarks

We would like to take the opportunity in the final part of this book to thank all those people who have supported us in writing it.

Let's begin with all those course participants over the years. On the one hand, they always motivated us to keep up-to-date with the sport, while on the other hand they were always asking us for a written training material.

We would also like to thank our relatives and friends, who stood by us giving advice and help. Their creative ideas, encouragement and improvement suggestions were a great help to us.

A big word of thanks also goes to our photographer – René Pintillie. With his innumerable photos, he made it possible for us to portray the sequence of movements for the throw pictorially almost like a video.

We must also thank Franz-Juergen Zeiser, our Chief Judge from the Baden Judo Association in Germany, for his support and for his invaluable work checking the texts in our book.

We send a hearty thank-you to Peter Frese, the President of the German Judo Association, for his 'Foreword' at the beginning of this book, as well as his encouraging support throughout and his successful work in identifying a good publisher.

Thanks also go to Doris Palermo, the President of our Club, for her words at the end of the book. Similarly, our thanks go to Norbert Nolte, the President of the Baden Judo Association for his continual words of encouragement.

A big, special thanks is, of course, due to our Judo instructor Alfredo Palermo. He has been extremely successful in getting us so enthused in the sport of Judo. It was through him that we took up the sport of Judo many years ago. Alfredo is not only a master and role model for us in Judo, but also a great friend and confidante.

Ute Pfeiffer
5th Dan

Guenther Bauer
3rd Dan

Photo & Illustration Credits

Cover Design: Sabine Groten
Cover Photo and Photos inside: René Pintillie

About the Authors

Ute Pfeiffer and Guenther Bauer have been members of the Sports Center in Ettlingen, Germany for over 30 years and were part of the founder members of the Judo Club in Ettlingen.

Following the conclusion of their activities in competition, they first started taking part in the Kata Championships in 1986. Although they were unable to regularly take part due to their busy private and business lives, besides gaining two fourth places, a third and a second place, they are able to look back on three Kata Championship titles in 1987, 1994 and 1996.

Since 1991, on behalf of Chief Judge Franz-Juergen Zeiser they have headed up the running of the Nage-no-Kata courses for the Baden Judo Association in Germany where they are often called on to officiate as judges for the Dan gradings.

Thanks to the innumerable photos and comprehensive texts, our two club members have been very successful in putting down on paper their knowledge and experience in the subject of Nage-no-Kata in an excellent and easily understandable manner.

We wish Ute and Guenther continuing success in the future – both in their sporting and private lives.

Doris Palermo
President of the Judo Club Ettlingen

September 1994 – The German Kata Championships
Ute Pfeiffer and Guenther Bauer with their instructor Alfredo Palermo